the Big Book of Children's Songs

ISBN 978-0-88188-942-0

HAL•LEONARD® CORPORATION

7777 W. BLUEMOUND RD. P.O. BOX 13819 MILWAUKEE, WI 53213

Contents

CATEGORICAL
The Big Book of Children's Songs

	ANIMALS	FINGER PLAYS	GAMES/MOVEMENT	HOLIDAYS	LANGUAGE DEVELOPMENT	NONSENSE	POP	QUIET TIME	ROUNDS	NURSERY RHYMES TRADITIONAL	VALUES
ALOUETTE					•				•	•T	
THE ALPHABET SONG		•	•		•					•T	
BIBBIDI-BOBBIDI-BOO						•	•				
B-I-N-G-O	•		•		•				•	•T	
BLUE TAIL FLY (Jimmy Crack Corn)	•									•T	
CAMPTOWN RACES	•									•T	
CHIM, CHIM, CHER-EE						•	•	•			•
CLEMENTINE										•T	•
DO-RE-MI			•		•		•	•			
A DREAM IS A WISH YOUR HEART MAKES							•	•			•
EENSY, WEENSY SPIDER	•	•			•			•		•N	
THE FARMER IN THE DELL	•		•		•					•T	
FRÉRE JACQUES (Brother John)					•			•		•T	•
FROSTY THE SNOWMAN				•			•				•
HAPPY BIRTHDAY TO YOU				•	•						
HEY, DIDDLE, DIDDLE	•				•	•	•			•N	
HICKORY, DICKORY, DOCK	•	•			•			•		•N	
HUMPTY DUMPTY					•	•				•N	
IT'S A SMALL WORLD							•	•			•
I'VE BEEN WORKING ON THE RAILROAD										•T	•
I WHISTLE A HAPPY TUNE					•		•				•
JACK AND JILL					•					•N	
JOHN JACOB JINGLEHEIMER SCHMIDT			•		•	•				•T	
LAVENDER BLUE (Dilly, Dilly)							•	•		•T	
LITTLE BO-PEEP	•				•					•N	
LITTLE BOY BLUE	•				•					•N	•
LITTLE MISS MUFFET					•					•N	
LONDON BRIDGE		•	•		•					•N	

CATEGORICAL
The Big Book of Children's Songs

	ANIMALS	FINGER PLAYS	GAMES/MOVEMENT	HOLIDAYS	LANGUAGE DEVELOPMENT	NONSENSE	POP	QUIET TIME	ROUNDS	NURSERY RHYMES TRADITIONAL	VALUES
MICKEY MOUSE MARCH	•		•		•	•					
THE MULBERRY BUSH	•		•							•T	
MY FAVORITE THINGS				•	•	•					•
OH! SUSANNA				•						•T	
OH WHERE, OH WHERE HAS MY LITTLE DOG GONE	•									•T	•
THE OLD GRAY MARE	•									•	•
OLD KING COLE					•					•N	
OLD MACDONALD HAD A FARM	•		•		•					•T	
ON TOP OF OLD SMOKY										•T	
PETER COTTONTAIL	•			•		•					
POLLY, WOLLY DOODLE			•		•					•T	
POP! GOES THE WEASEL	•		•							•T	
THE RAINBOW CONNECTION						•	•				•
RED RIVER VALLEY										•T	•
RING AROUND THE ROSIE			•		•				•	•T	
ROW, ROW, ROW YOUR BOAT			•						•	•T	
SCHOOL DAYS						•					•
SHE'LL BE COMIN' 'ROUND THE MOUNTAIN			•							•T	
SKIP TO MY LOU			•							•T	
SUPERCALIFRAGILISTICEXPIALIDOCIOUS					•	•	•				
TEN LITTLE INDIANS		•			•					•T	
THIS LAND IS YOUR LAND						•					•
THIS OLD MAN (Nick Nack Paddy Wack)	•		•		•					•T	
THREE BLIND MICE	•				•				•	•N	
TWINKLE, TWINKLE LITTLE STAR		•			•				•	•N	
YANKEE DOODLE			•	•						•T	
YELLOW SUBMARINE						•					•

Parents, Teachers, Leaders...

Music is a basic joy of life. To encourage and promote that joy, these songs provide the elements that make up the child's world of music. The categories listed below provide you with direction for a variety of musical and learning experiences when you're planning activities for children.

Animal, Holiday and Nonsense Songs

Encourage children to use their imagination to act out movements of songs. They can be a bunny one minute and a train the next. Children can use visualization to create story-songs in their minds.

Language Development

Is appropriate for all children from infants up, but is especially useful for children whose primary language is other than English. A most important aspect of any child's education is the fostering of a positive self-image. For instance, when learning *Happy Birthday To You*, a child learns that it's his or her special day and that he or she is unique.

Values

When preparing children to make appropriate choices in today's society, it's imperative that they be given opportunites to explore their attitudes and compare them with attitudes of other people. For instance, *I've Been Working On The Railroad* shows the value of working hard and being rewarded by seeing the fruits of one's labor. *The Rainbow Connection* talks about all the colors of people throughout the world. *This Land Is Your Land* points out how we all share this country and its wonders.

Games and Finger Play

These activities stimulate involvement by integrating movement and vocalization. For younger children, the actions precede the vocabulary of the song, and through repetition instill the concept. For *FINGER PLAY* songs, the children pantomime the key words of the songs—forming the shapes with their hands. These are wonderful for situations where children can't leave their seats, such as in the car or if they're confined to a wheelchair or bed.

GAMES & FINGER PLAY

The Alphabet Song

Make or buy alphabet flash cards and have each child hold them up as their letter(s) is sung. **Finger Play:** Children trace the shape of each letter in the air with their index finger.

B-i-n-g-o

Each time the song is sung, replace an additional letter in Bingo's name with a clap, a bark, a sound or silence, until all letters are replaced.

Do-Re-Mi

Draw a big music staff and name the notes of the scale. Have children point to each scale step as it's sung. Assign each portion of the song to a different child (as they did in the movie). Make up movements to follow the lyric.

The Farmer in the Dell

Children form a circle, the leader (farmer) stands in the center and chooses a *wife* who moves into the center. The *wife* chooses a nurse, etc., until everyone's formed an inner circle and *the cheese stands alone*. Add or delete verses depending on the number of children.

John Jacob Jingleheimer Schmidt

Repeat this song until everyone falls over. First, sing it very loud, then medium, then soft, whisper and finally just "mouth" the lyric. **Finger Play:** Follow the lyric and have the children point to themselves when the song says *his name is my name too*. Then point *out*, and finally, cup their hands around their mouths when the song *shouts*.

London Bridge

Two children form a bridge with their arms, the other children march through the bridge until the phrase "*My fair lady*," at which point they trap that person in their arms and that person joins them, becoming part of the bridge. **Finger Play:** In the first verse, children hold their hands up and form a bridge with their fingers, then lower them in time with the music. Verse 2, they build up the bridge with bars, alternating hands. Verse 3, they bend and break the bars. Verse 4, they pretend that they're building, silver with their right hand, gold with their left.

Mickey Mouse March

This is a good song to teach the marching step and the concept of rhythm. When the children are marching, have them bring their knees up slightly and step down lightly! Emphasize the rhythm—ONE, two.

The Mulberry Bush

Form a circle and move to the left on the chorus. Act out the lyric in each of the verses. Children can also make up actions, such as *This is the way we wash the car, bang the drums*, etc. **Finger Play:** Trace circles in the air, do the activities in each verse with just the hands.

Old MacDonald Had a Farm

Be sure to sing all the animal sounds of each verse when you add a new one. Add more animals. **Finger Play:** Children can make faces to imitate the different animals; form their hands or fingers into big ears for the donkey, make a pug nose for the pig, move their heads like a chicken.

Polly, Wolly, Doodle

Children form a circle and move to the left in a shuffle step or a fast walk. Make up movements to follow the lyric.

Pop! Goes the Weasel

Finger Play: Use key words for forming movements. Have children make a circle with their fingers for "*All around the cobbler's bench...*" "*chase*" their fingers, sew with the needle, and drop their money. Then, clap their hands or snap their fingers each time "*Pop! Goes the Weasel*" is sung.

Ring Around the Rosie

Everyone forms a circle and moves to the left; children can fall or sit on "*...all fall down.*" Be sure the surface is soft.

Row, Row, Row Your Boat

Along with singing this song endlessly as a round, children can also sit down or stand up whenever they start singing the "*Row, row, row*" section. Make up movements to follow the lyric. See the additional "Suggested Activity" at the end of the music.

She'll Be Comin' Round the Mountain

This is a traditional square dance. Children can make up new verses. Make up movements to follow the lyric.

Skip to My Lou

Older children choose partners and skip to the music. Younger children can form a circle and just walk or bounce.

This Old Man

Follow the instructions in the song and make up movement patterns for each verse (to suit the level of development of the children). **Finger Play:** For each verse, children can form the shape of, or point to the key object, such as the door, a hive, etc.

Yankee Doodle

Another good song to teach the marching step and the concept of rhythm. When the children are marching, have them bring their knees up slightly and step down lightly! Emphasize the rhythm—ONE, two. Make up movements to follow the lyric.

THE ALPHABET SONG

ALOUETTE

Oh, a - lou-et - te, gen - tille a - lou-et - te;

A - lou-et - te, je te plu - me-rai. A - lou-et - te,

gen - tille a - lou-et - te; A - lou-et - te, je te plu - me-rai.

Je te plu - me-rai la têt'; je te plu - me - rai la tet'.

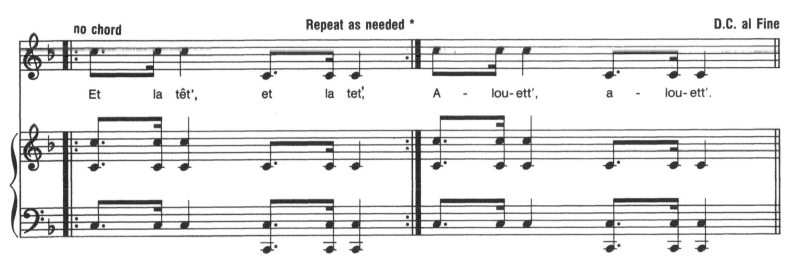

Et la têt', et la tet', A - lou-ett', a - lou-ett'.

no chord   **Repeat as needed ***   **D.C. al Fine**

*Each chorus adds a new part of the body, in reverse order. For example, Chorus 3 is sung:

Et le nez, et le nez,
Et le bec, et le bec,
Et la têt', et le têt',
Alouett', Alouett'.
Oh, *etc.*

2. le bec *(beak)*
3. le nez *(nose)*
4. les yeux *(eyes)*
5. le cou *(neck)*

6. les ailes *(wings)*
7. le dos *(back)*
8. les pattes *(feet)*
9. la queue *(tail)*

BINGO

NOTE: Each time a letter of BINGO is deleted in the lyric, clap your hands in place of singing the letter.

BIBBIDI-BOBBIDI-BOO
(From Walt Disney's "CINDERELLA")

Words by JERRY LIVINGSTON
Music by MACK DAVID and AL HOFFMAN

Sa - la - ga - doo - la men-chic-ka boo - la bib-bi-di-bob-bi-di-boo Put 'em to-geth-er and what have you got bib-bi-di-bob-bi-di-boo.

Sa - la - ga - doo - la men-chic-ka boo - la bib-bi-di-bob-bi-di-boo. It-'ll do mag-ic be-lieve it or not,

THE BLUE-TAIL FLY
(JIMMY CRACK CORN)

2. And when he'd ride in the afternoon,
   I'd follow with a hickory broom;
   The pony being very shy,
   Got bitten by a blue-tail fly.
   Chorus:

3. One day he rode around the farm,
   The flies so numerous, they did swarm,
   One chanced to bite him on the thigh,
   The devil take the blue-tail fly.
   Chorus:

4. The pony run, he jump, he pitch,
   He threw old Master in a ditch;
   He died and the jury wondered why
   The verdict was the blue-tail fly.
   Chorus:

5. They laid him under a 'simmon tree,
   His epitaph is there to see;
   "Beneath the earth I'm forced to lie,
   A victim of the blue-tail fly."
   Chorus:

Alternate Verses

2. We went riding one afternoon,
   I followed with a hickory broom,
   The pony being very shy,
   Got bitten by a blue-tail fly.
   Chorus:

3. The pony he did rear and pitch,
   He threw old Master in a ditch;
   The jury asked the reason why,
   The verdict was the blue-tail fly.
   Chorus:

4. So we laid old Master down to rest;
   And on a stone this last request:
   "Beneath the earth I'm forced to lie,
   A victim of the blue-tail fly."
   Chorus:

CAMPTOWN RACES

CHIM CHIM CHER-EE
(From Walt Disney's "MARY POPPINS")

Words and Music by RICHARD M. SHERMAN
and ROBERT B. SHERMAN

CLEMENTINE

DO-RE-MI
(From "THE SOUND OF MUSIC")

Words by OSCAR HAMMERSTEIN II
Music by RICHARD RODGERS

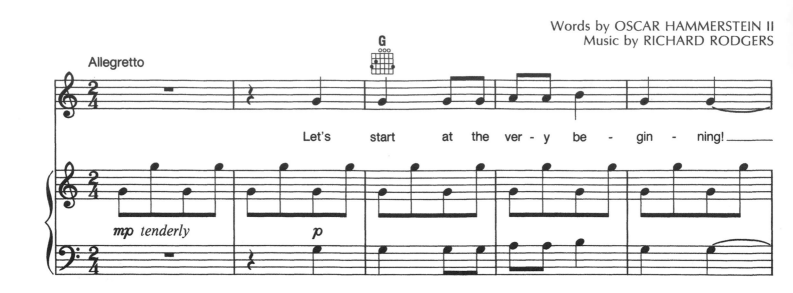

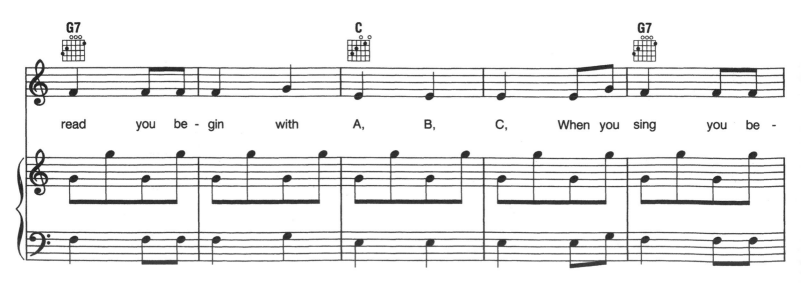

28

A Dream Is A Wish Your Heart Makes

(From Walt Disney's "CINDERELLA")

Words and Music by MACK DAVID,
AL HOFFMAN and JERRY LIVINGSTON

A dream is a wish your heart makes ____ When your fast a- sleep. ____ In dreams you will

EENSY WEENSY SPIDER

THE FARMER IN THE DELL

3. The wife takes a child, etc.

4. The child takes a nurse, etc.

5. The nurse takes a dog, etc.

6. The dog takes a cat, etc.

7. The cat takes a rat, etc.

8. The rat takes the cheese, etc.

9. The cheese stands alone, etc.

FRÈRE JACQUES

FROSTY THE SNOW MAN

Words and Music by STEVE NELSON
and JACK ROLLINS

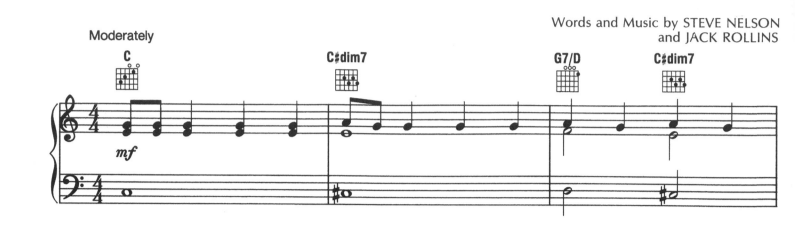

Frost - y the snow man was a
Frost - y the snow man knew the

jol - ly hap - py soul,   With a corn cob pipe and a
sun was hot that day,   So he said "Let's run and we'll

HAPPY BIRTHDAY TO YOU

Words and Music by MILDRED J. HILL
and PATTY S. HILL

HEY, DIDDLE, DIDDLE

Lively

Hey, did - dle, did - dle! The cat and the fid - dle, The cow jumped o - ver the moon; The lit - tle dog laughed To see such sport And the dish ran a - way with the spoon.

HICKORY DICKORY DOCK

HUMPTY DUMPTY

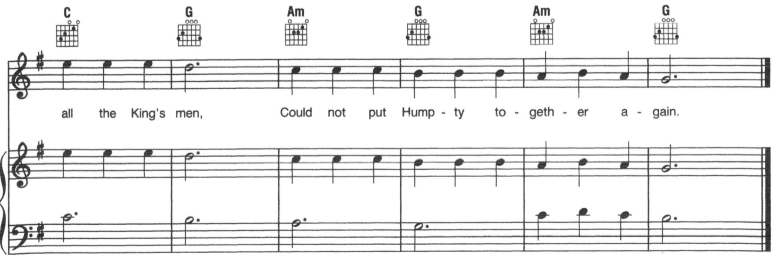

I WHISTLE A HAPPY TUNE

(From "The King And I")

Words by OSCAR HAMMERSTEIN II
Music by RICHARD RODGERS

I'VE BEEN WORKING ON THE RAILROAD

IT'S A SMALL WORLD

(Theme from The Disneyland and Walt Disney World Attraction, "IT'S A SMALL WORLD")

Words and Music by RICHARD M. SHERMAN
AND ROBERT B. SHERMAN

March Tempo

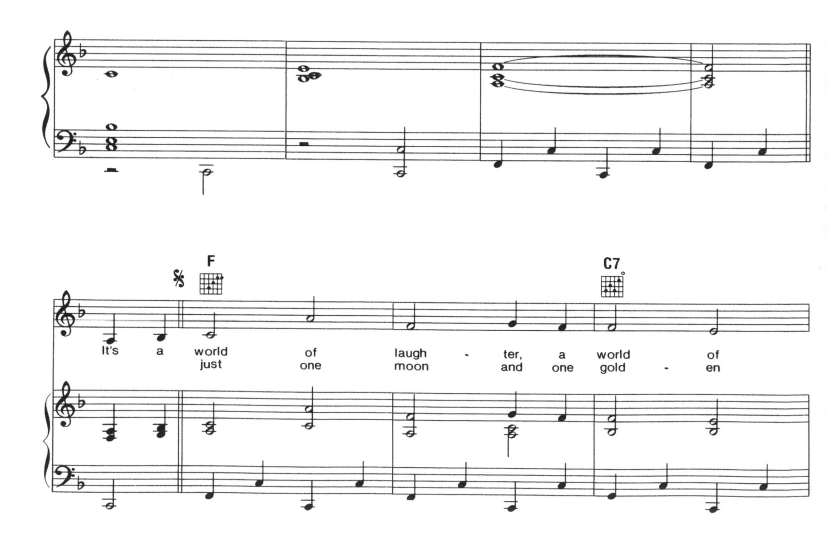

It's a world of laugh - ter, a world of
just one moon and one world gold - en

JACK AND JILL

LAVENDER BLUE
(Dilly Dilly)

Words by LARRY MOREY
Music by ELIOT DANIEL

Lav - en - der's blue, dil - ly, dil - ly, Lav - en - der's green, When I am king, dil - ly, dil - ly, You shall be queen. Call up your

Some to make hay, dilly, dilly,
Some to cut corn,
While you and I, dilly, dilly,
Keep ourselves warm.

JOHN JACOB JINGLEHEIMER SCHMIDT

LITTLE BO PEEP

Additional Lyrics for LITTLE BO PEEP

3. Then up she took her little crook,
Determined for to find them;
She found them indeed, but it made her heart bleed,
For they'd left their tails behind them.

4. It happened one day, as Bo-Peep did stray
Unto a meadow hard by;
There she espied their tails, side by side,
All hung on a tree to dry.

5. She heaved a sigh, and wiped her eye,
And ran o'er hill and dale,
And tried what she could, as a shepherdess should,
To tack each sheep to its tail.

THE MULBERRY BUSH

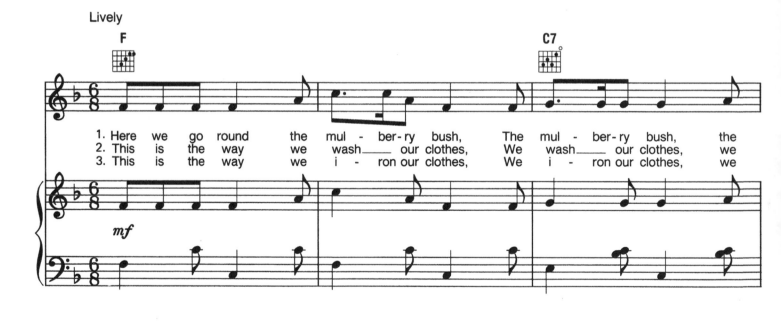

1. Here we go round the mul-ber-ry bush, The mul-ber-ry bush, the
2. This is the way we wash our clothes, We wash our clothes, we
3. This is the way we i-ron our clothes, We i-ron our clothes, we

mul-ber-ry bush. Here we go round the mul-ber-ry bush So
wash our clothes. This is the way we wash our clothes So
i-ron our clothes. This is the way we i-ron our clothes So

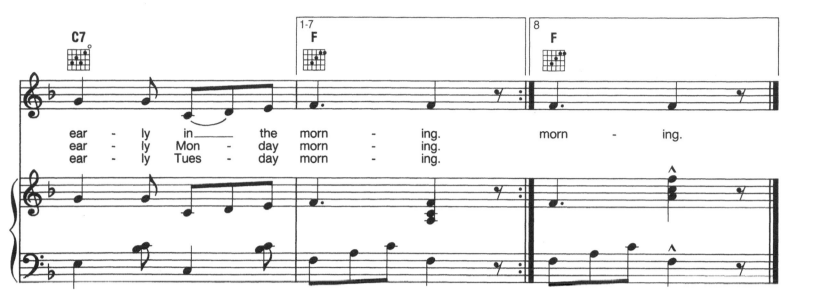

early in the morning.
early Monday morning.
early Tuesday morning.

morning.

4. This is the way we scrub the floor, *etc.*
So early Wednesday morning.

5. This is the way we mend our clothes, *etc.*
So early Thursday morning.

6. This is the way we sweep the house, *etc.*
So early Friday morning.

7. This is the way we bake our bread, *etc.*
So early Saturday morning.

8. This is the way we go to church, *etc.*
So early Sunday morning.

LITTLE BOY BLUE

LITTLE MISS MUFFET

LONDON BRIDGE

3. Iron bars will bend and break,
   Bend and break, bend and break;
   Iron bars will bend and break,
   My fair lady.

4. Build it up with gold and silver,
   Gold and silver, gold and silver;
   Build it up with gold and silver,
   My fair lady.

MICKEY MOUSE MARCH

Words and Music by
JIMMIE DODD

Additional Interludes

5. We have fun and we play safely!
6. Look both ways when you cross crossings!
7. Don't take chances! Play with safety!
8. When you ride your bike be careful!
9. Play a little, work a little.

10. Sing a song while you are working!
11. It will make your burden lighter.
12. Do a good turn for your neighbor.
13. You can learn things while you're playing.
14. It's a lot of fun to learn things.

MY FAVORITE THINGS
(From "THE SOUND OF MUSIC")

Words by OSCAR HAMMERSTEIN II
Music by RICHARD RODGERS

OH, SUSANNA

THE OLD GRAY MARE

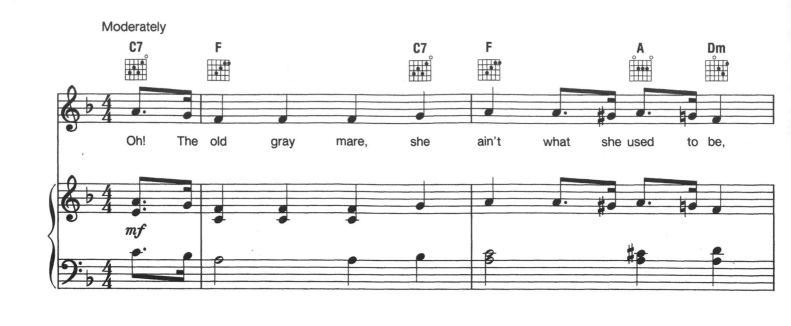

Oh! The old gray mare, she ain't what she used to be,

ain't what she used to be, Ain't what she used to be, the

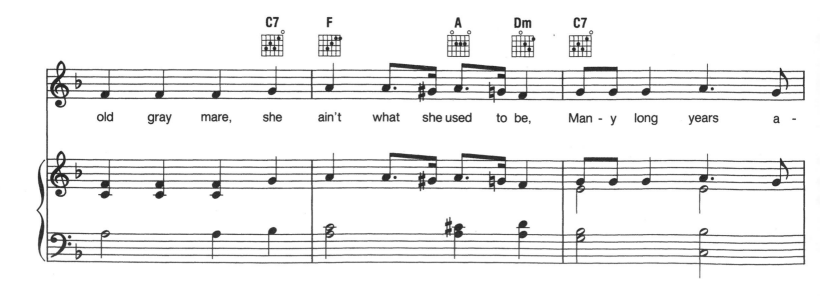

old gray mare, she ain't what she used to be, Man-y long years a-

OLD KING COLE

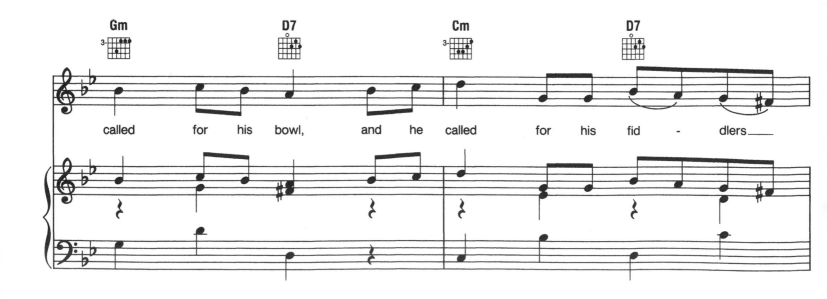

OLD MacDONALD HAD A FARM

4. Old MacDonald had a farm,
   E-I-E-I-O,
   And on his farm he had a horse,
   E-I-E-I-O,
   With a neigh-neigh here and a neigh-neigh there, *etc.*

5. Old MacDonald had a farm,
   E-I-E-I-O,
   And on his farm he had a donkey,
   E-I-E-I-O,
   With a hee-haw here, *etc.*

6. Old MacDonald had a farm,
   E-I-E-I-O,
   And on his farm he had some chickens,
   E-I-E-I-O,
   With a chick-chick here, *etc.*

For additional verses, add your own animals.

ON TOP OF OLD SMOKY

Moderately waltz

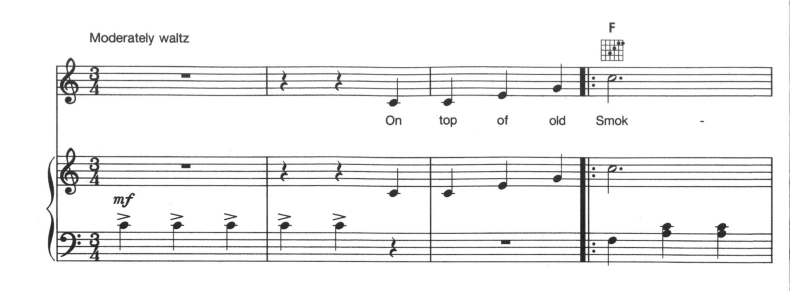

On top of old Smok -

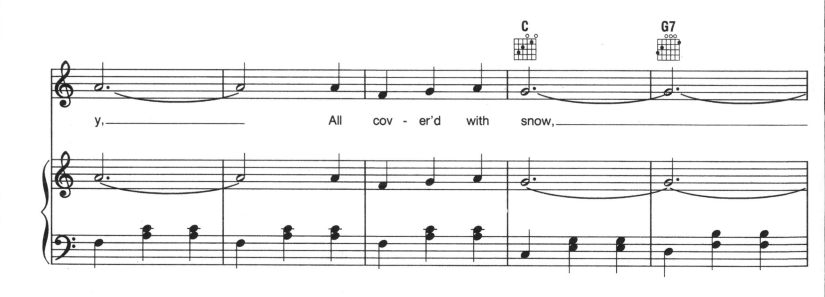

y, _____ All cov - er'd with snow, _____

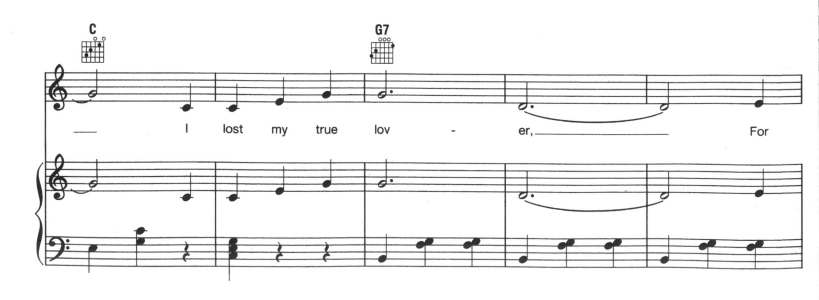

_____ I lost my true lov - er, _____ For

court - in' too slow._____ 2. *(see additional lyrics)*

skies._____

2. A-courtin's a pleasure,
A-flirtin's a grief,
A false-hearted lover -
Is worse than a thief.

3. For a thief, he will rob you,
And take what you have,
But a false-hearted lover -
Sends you to your grave.

4. She'll hug you and kiss you,
And tell you more lies,
Than the ties on the railroad,
Or the stars in the skies.

PETER COTTONTAIL

Words and Music by STEVE NELSON
and JACK ROLLINS

Easter Version
1. Here comes Pe - ter Cot - ton - tail,
2. Here comes Pe - ter Cot - ton - tail,

Year 'Round Version
1. Look at Pe - ter Cot - ton - tail,
2. Lit - tle Pe - ter Cot - ton - tail,

Hop - pin' down the bun - ny trail,___ Hip - pi - ty hop - pin',
Hop - pin' down the bun - ny trail,___ Look at him stop, and
Hop - pin' down the bun - ny trail,___ A rab - bit of dis -
Hop - pin' down the bun - ny trail,___ Hap - pened to stop for

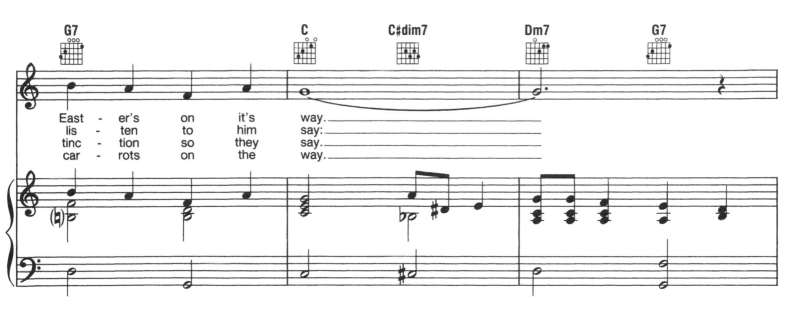

Easter's on it's way. _____
lis - ten to him say: _____
tinc - tion so him they say. _____
car - rots on the way. _____

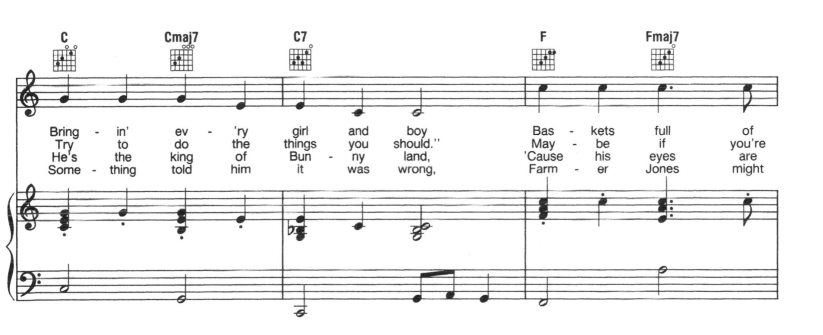

Bring - in' ev - 'ry girl and boy Bas - kets full of
Try to do the the girl things you should." May - be full if you're
He's the king of Bun - ny land, 'Cause his eyes are
Some - thing told him it was wrong, Farm - er Jones might

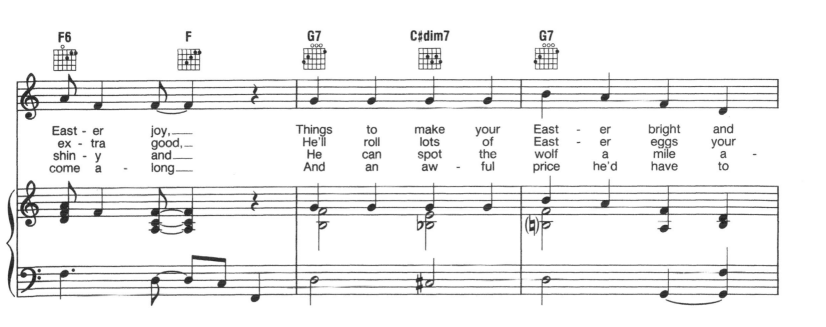

East - er joy, ___ Things to make your East - er bright and
ex - tra good, ___ He'll roll lots of East - er eggs your
shin - y and ___ He can spot the wolf a mile a -
come a - long ___ And an aw - ful price he'd have to

gay.\
way.\
way.\
pay.

He's got jel-ly beans for Tom-my, Col-ored\
You'll wake up on East-er morn-ing And you'll\
When the oth-ers go for clo-ver And the\
But he knew his legs were fast-er So he

eggs for sis-ter Sue,\
know for that he was there.\
big bad wolf three or four\
nib-bled three or four

There's an or-chid for your\
When you find those choc-'late\
He's the one that's watch-ing\
And he al-most met dis-

Mom-my And an East-er bon-net, too. Oh!\
bun-nies That he's hid-ing ev-'ry-where. Oh!\
o-ver Giv-in' sig-nals with his ears. And\
as-ter When he heard that shot-gun roar. Oh,

POLLY WOLLY DOODLE

4. Oh, I went to bed, but it wasn't no use,
   Singing polly-wolly-doodle all the day.
   My feet stuck out like a chicken roost,
   Singing polly-wolly-doodle all the day.
   Chorus

5. Behind the barn down on my knees,
   Singing polly-wolly-doodle all the day.
   I thought I heard a chicken sneeze,
   Singing polly-wolly-doodle all the day.
   Chorus

6. He sneezed so hard with the whooping cough,
   Singing polly-wolly-doodle all the day.
   He sneezed his head and tail right off,
   Singing polly-wolly-doodle all the day.
   Chorus

POP GOES THE WEASEL

OH WHERE, OH WHERE HAS MY LITTLE DOG GONE?

Oh where, oh where has my lit-tle dog gone? Oh where, oh

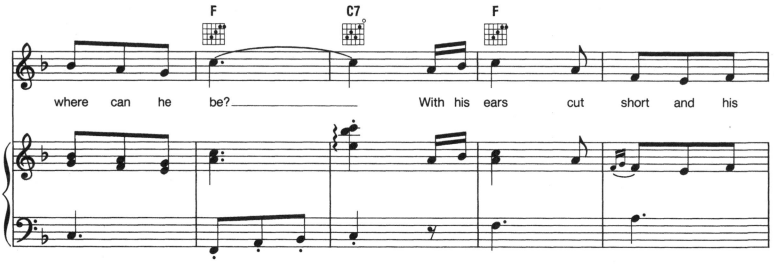

where can he be?_____ With his ears cut short and his

tail cut long; Oh where, oh where can he be?_____

THE RAINBOW CONNECTION

By PAUL WILLIAMS and
KENNETH L. ASCHER

Moderately, with a lilt

Why are there so man-y songs a-bout rain-bows, and
Who said that ev-'ry wish would be heard and an-swered and when

what's on the oth - er side? _____
wished on the morn - ing star? _____

Rain-bows are vis - ions, ____ but on-ly il - lu - sions, And
Some-bod - y thought of that, and some-one be - lieved it;

95

RED RIVER VALLEY

while.
way.
me.
Come and sit by my

side if you love me._____ Do not

hast - en to bid me a - dieu.

RING AROUND THE ROSIE

Brightly

Ring a-round the ros - y, a pock-et full of po - sies;

ash - es, ash - es, we all fall down.

Lit - tle Sal - ly Wa - ters, sit - ting in a sau - cer,

ROW, ROW, ROW YOUR BOAT

Mer - ri - ly, mer - ri - ly, mer - ri - ly, mer - ri - ly, Life is but a dream.

A SUGGESTED ACTIVITY

"Row, Row, Row Your Boat" is a famous "round" that has been sung and enjoyed by people of all ages. When sung correctly, the melody actually goes around and around. Here's how it works: The singers are divided into two groups. The first group sings the first line alone. At this point, the second group starts at the beginning, while the first group continues with the second line. In this manner, the groups are always exactly one line apart as the tune is repeated. The last time through, the second group sings the final line alone just as the first group sang the opening line alone. Try it . . . it's fun!

SCHOOL-DAYS

SHE'LL BE COMIN' 'ROUND THE MOUNTAIN

3. Oh, we'll all go to meet her when she comes,
   Oh, we'll all go to meet her when she comes,
   Oh, we'll all go to meet her,
   Oh, we'll all go to meet her,
   Oh, we'll all go to meet her when she comes.

4. We'll be singin' "Hallelujah" when she comes,
   We'll be singin' "Hallelujah" when she comes,
   We'll be singin' "Hallelujah,"
   We'll be singin' "Hallelujah,"
   We'll be singin' "Hallelujah" when she comes.

SKIP TO MY LOU

2. I'll find another one, prettier than you,
   I'll find another one, prettier than you,
   I'll find another one, prettier than you,
   Skip to my Lou, my darling.

3. Little red wagon, painted blue.

4. Can't get a red bird, a blue bird'll do.

5. Cows in the meadow, moo, moo, moo.

6. Flies in the buttermilk, shoo, shoo, shoo.

SUPERCALIFRAGILISTICEXPIALIDOCIOUS

(From Walt Disney's "MARY POPPINS")

Words and Music by RICHARD M. SHERMAN
and ROBERT B. SHERMAN

MARY POPPINS
Sup - er - cal - i - frag - il - is - tic - ex - pi - al - i - do - cious!

E - ven though the sound of it is some - thing quite a - tro - cious,

If you say it loud e - nough, you'll al - ways sound pre - co - cious.

TEN LITTLE INDIANS

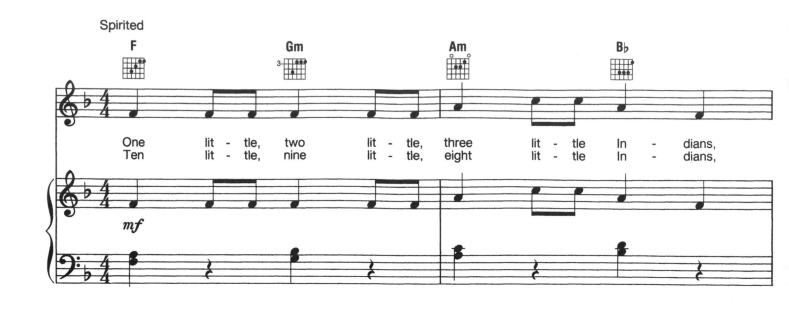

One lit-tle, two lit-tle, three lit-tle In-dians,
Ten lit-tle, nine lit-tle, eight lit-tle In-dians,

Four lit-tle, five lit-tle, six lit-tle In-dians, Seven lit-tle, eight lit-tle,
Seven lit-tle, six lit-tle, five lit-tle In-dians, Four lit-tle, three lit-tle,

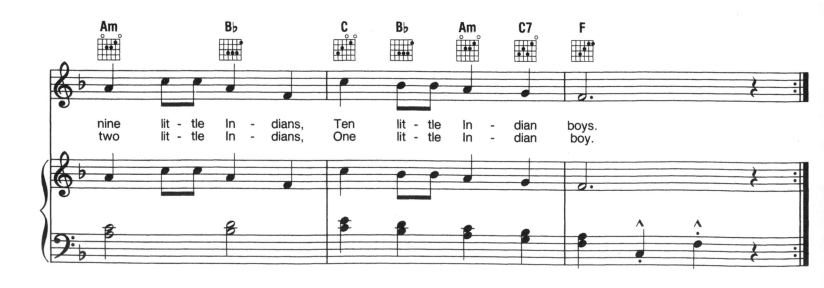

nine lit-tle In-dians, Ten lit-tle In-dian boys.
two lit-tle In-dians, One lit-tle In-dian boy.

THIS OLD MAN

*Two . . . . on the shoe
*Three . . . on the tree
*Four . . . . on the door
*Five . . . . on the hive
*Six . . . . . on the sticks
*Seven . . . up in heaven
*Eight . . . on the gate
*Nine . . . . on the line
*Ten . . . . . once again

THIS LAND IS YOUR LAND

Words and Music by WOODY GUTHRIE

4. When the sun came shining, and I was strolling,
   And the wheat fields waving and the dust clouds rolling,
   As the fog was lifting a voice was chanting:
   This land was made for you and me.

5. As I went walking, I saw a sign there,
   And on the sign it said "No Trespassing."
   But on the other side it didn't say nothing,
   That side was made for you and me.

6. In the shadow of the steeple I saw my people,
   By the relief office I seen my people;
   As they stood there hungry, I stood there asking
   Is this land made for you and me?

7. Nobody living can ever stop me,
   As I go walking that freedom highway;
   Nobody living can ever make me turn back,
   This land was made for you and me.

TWINKLE, TWINKLE, LITTLE STAR

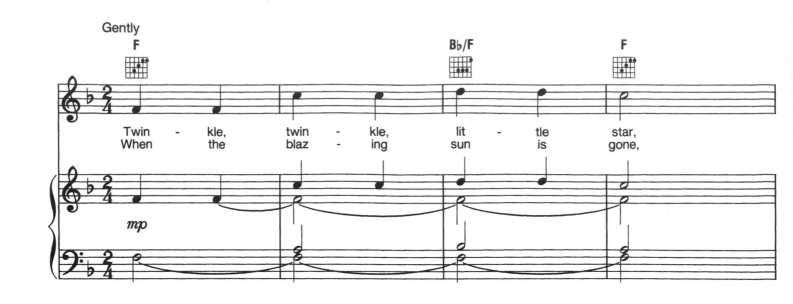

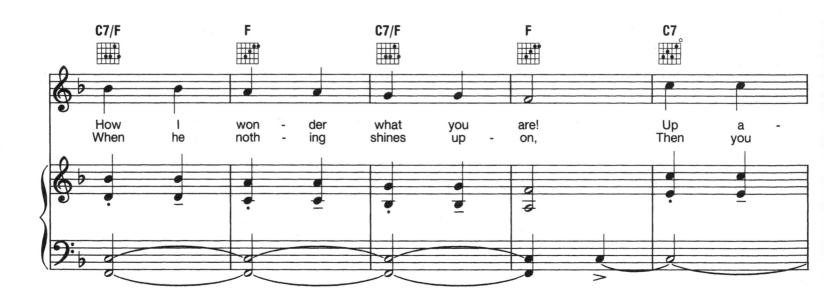

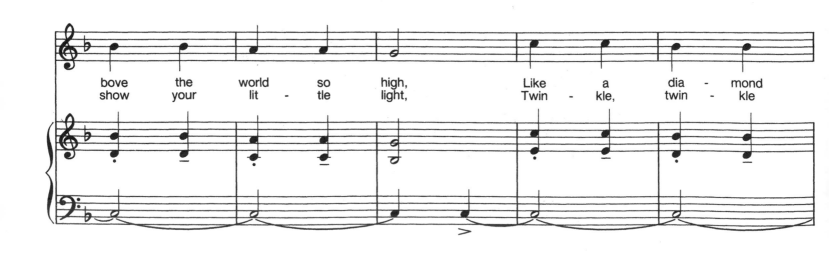

in the sky. } all the night.

Twin - kle, twin - kle, lit - tle star,

How I won - der what you are!

Parody

Starkle, starkle, little twink,
How I wonder what you think!
Up above the world so high,
Think you own the whole darn sky?
Starkle, starkle, little twink,
You're not so great,
That's what I think!

YELLOW SUBMARINE

Words and Music by
JOHN LENNON and PAUL McCARTNEY

Chorus:

THREE BLIND MICE

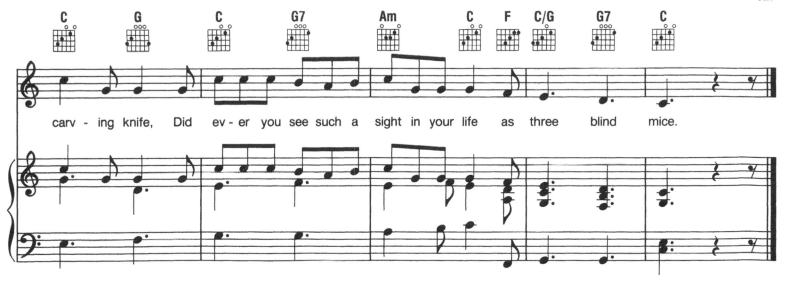

YANKEE DOODLE